Anthem

With love
to one of the
most powerful
women I've know
beso, Nanci

ANTHEM
HELEN HUMPHREYS

Brick Books

CANADIAN CATALOGUING IN PUBLICATION DATA

Humphreys, Helen, 1961–
  Anthem

Poems.

ISBN 1-894078-02-0

1. Title.

PS8565.U558A87 1999   C811'.54   C99-931042-9
PR9199.3.H852A67 1999

We acknowledge the support of the Canada Council for the Arts for our publishing programme. The support of the Ontario Arts Council is also gratefully acknowledged.

Photograph of the author is by Jerry Bauer.

Typeset in Trump Mediaeval; the stock is acid-free Zephyr Antique laid. Printed and bound by the Porcupine's Quill Inc.

Brick Books,
431 Boler Road, Box 20081,
London, Ontario, N6K 4G6

brick.books@sympatico.ca

Contents

Bluewater

Three girls on the rail track. I'm the one
in the middle. Sun wobbles through trees. The sisters
smoke and swear. It's no one's fault
that our mothers are friends, we all know and don't

know this. The younger sister sucks cocks
for money. And sometimes for free, she says, and
laughs. By the time we get to the water it's night
and the bridge is a huge, shiny staple arched over dark,

crumpled riverbanks. This is where you come
to die, says the older sister. We stand in the mud
under steel crosses, look for bodies
bumping in the current. Bluewater bridge. We can't see

the colour of the water. The bridge is silver. Going
back, a spike of moonlight through our thin chests.
The older sister holds my hand all the way, without
my asking. Next year, when she is seventeen, she will plunge

from the hood of a moving car. Skull wired together,
teeth gone. Brain damage, skin grafts, someone else's
rebuilt face. The younger sister will marry
a man who hates her, have children, find

god. Head tilted back, she will take the
lord's body into her mouth, again and again, pray
for a part of her life to start or stop or
be revealed. This is how

faith happens, sanctifying what the body remembers.
Our bodies that have trusted what touched them, what
they were taught to touch. Something fills our mouths –
the flesh, the word (holy, holy). There is space
above the moving dark to fly through. Believe this.
There is the shaky knot of hand in human hand.

Beneath the Sea

Down under water a flicker
through murky glass. Snag
in the throat. Murmur.
My hand slick on the steel
wall. Words rising bubbles
from the diver. Flutter
across the tank. In his arms
blossom of octopus. Here

we are, sway of lost to found,
back again. Language and
love. What we say, a wave
of tentacles. What we want.
My breath opaque on the glass.
We're our own ghosts already
in the watery dark.
Fish. Swimming.

By Definition

The girl next door takes her clothes off
for us. She calls it *putting on a show*,
stands on a beer box in the garage
flicking her thin body from side to side,
getting tangled in the T-shirt she pulls up and over
her head. She never wants to play anything else
and we walk from her, fists full of trolls
with purple hair. Boring, we say to each other.
It is so, so boring.

We do it ourselves, once in a while, lie down naked
on the hard dirt between the houses, let the twins
across the road examine us. Because in the
hot, slack sun, buzz of summer, we know we must be
dying of something. We can feel it sticking in our chests,
the way our bike tires clutch and slip on gravel.
The slow slide just before we go down.

Years later, visiting these houses we grew up in, we
will say to our mothers, He took her on business
trips. She was ten years old. And because there is
a name now we will name it. Standing by the back door,
watching rain braid on the glass.

The word never explains the thing. Naming
is relational – this did or did not happen. It fails
the experience, doesn't call up a child's knowing,
that place where words are the far shore and we are floating
away from them. How we sensed she had crossed over. How
we smelled her father on her, and what we minded was
her defection from childhood. What we minded
was her leaving us behind.

Installation

What we make doesn't recover from us.
Twisted scaffold, trellis of rust. This
is how we will be gone. The steel hull
grinning with rivets. Shiny notes of chrome
swinging from the stave of the wrecker's wall.

Those we loved and nothing for that. The moon
a chalk circle over dark harbour.
Old rail tracks slippery under my feet.
Broken ladder on the tanker. My breath
ascending the rungs of air. I have

been here, lived in this place, loved you.
There's a snarl of wire on white sand.
Plastic bottles nested in tall grasses
by the channel mouth. We are survived by these
shapes, by the shape of our lives without us.

This Far

Over the bridge. The iron railing.
Darkness plunges in slow, sad arcs
into the river below.
Nothing on the radio, just the tick
of a stone in the tire, the miles of it
wearing down. Imagined blue, that's
the sound of loss. Blue stone.

What are the things that make us
feel like who we are? Voices
in a room. A place to come from,
the bright, glittering wash of a city.
Landscape spliced to language.
Roads we know.

There's a stutter of light in the hall
behind us. Put on your coat, I say.
Dawn sticky red over the long cant of roofs.
The car door salted with frost. This is how
I come back, and leave, and never go.

Narrative

I'm here, she says. Come for me.
Then a truck goes by and the rest
is a hiss of air brakes and water. It's raining
where she is (was) and it's raining now
(which is why I put the rain in)
and I imagine the truck is from Canadian Tire
because we counted once and they have
more trucks on the highway than anyone else.
(The 401 – Toronto to Montreal and back again.)

Already this scene is gone. The words
are associative, not descriptive. They slide right out
from under us. I can't tell you anything
and this is my story. Is it raining where you are?
Are you watching? Is the rain the story now?

It's you on the phone and the truck going by is
the poem – not this one – but the one we both wanted
it to be, what we wanted from it. Music
and meaning. The clear notes of the rain.
A word that beetles down the glass alone, dodges other words.
A singularity. Experience and its given name.

I'm still here, she says. What's taking you so long?

Variations

Music comes undone.

Shimmer of rain in the trees like the
shiver of blood in my chest.

These things happen in 4/4 time: walking,
the moving wings of geese overhead,
beating of the human heart.

The slow-motion lurch of leaving. Touching
your life with the flat of your hand.
These walls. This book. Memory as prophesy.

The notes of the piano released up, showering
down. A word is not pure sound like that, cannot

persuade the air to change.

Chinchilla

1.
A man cries downstairs in our kitchen.
His girlfriend runs from him. I heard
the slack and spring of the front door, my mother
calling *Jaimie*, just once.

Through my bedroom window I can see the figure
moving across the field, flat black flag of night
pinned crooked to her chest. She's a daughter of my
mother's friend. They live hundreds of miles from here.

It turns out she ran away and her boyfriend, unable
to stop her, drove her instead. My mother
blows up the air bed in the basement with the
foot pump and he comes down, still crying, talks

about wanting to marry her, about starting
a chinchilla farm to pay for the wedding
and the house they'd need. But she still won't say yes.
Air spurts out of the pump – no, no, no. My mother

sends me for Jaimie and I walk out, in my pyjamas,
into the secret, sudden night. She's standing
by the marshy bit, the shallow pond we find in springtime.
Her knees are wet, like she's fallen or gone down.
They want you back, I say.

2.

Any story we remember is a truth about ourselves.
What has happened to us never really stops happening.
It is always dark. I am leading a woman
out of this. Later I will be this woman,
will make good men cry. Later still
I will want to have this woman. Without
the story, is real life possible?

3.

This is what I have remembered, all of it
suspect. I'm lying to you. Please believe me.
A man cries. A woman runs from him. She can't
run forever, everyone knows this. A man cries
because a woman runs from him, because she wants
to run instead of letting him try to make her happy.
Everyone knows he will fail to make her happy.

4.

The man was crying and no man had cried in our house before.

The woman was running and grown-ups never ran.

The air bed, used only for camping, was out
of context. Pyjamas were for indoors. My mother
wasn't calling my name. I said
the words for the first time that I would
repeat over and over in my adult life.
I want you. I want you back.

The chinchillas were the thing that couldn't be imagined.
A fur coat cut and sewn back into an animal.
Farmed, like wheat or corn. Fed as usual
one day, slaughtered the next. A crop
of blood and skin. Harvest. Chinchilla.
Love is death. Run from it.

For Jackie, Who Will Never Read This

Saturdays we have dinner in her booth. Red
table cloth. Food she's brought to the car wash
from across town. Lasagna. One week fried chicken.

We sit in our uniforms at the counter, wedged
between the safe and cash register. Lights out.
Waxy splash of candles making
the booth look adrift from outside.

I turned back once at the pumps,
helping some woman with her gas cap and saw
the lit bubble of it behind me on the asphalt.
Signal, I thought. Lighthouse. Ship at sea.
I came in and told her these things,
but she wasn't interested. Listen,
she said, pouring coke into two plastic cups.
My boyfriend is fucking useless. Doesn't
do shit. *Won't* do shit. Like those guys.
Like they say on TV. Emotionally reversed.
Reserved, I said. Shut up,
she said. You know what I mean.

I knew what she meant only because I knew her. Dragging
the ladder over the parking lot on Monday
morning, scrape of it against concrete, because
she's left a note stuck to my stool with gum:
The cube sign isn't revolting.
My body pressed to the steel, hands up
under the plastic skirt. Turn
you bastard. Rotate, swivel, twist, spin.
Pirouette your sad dance of light around this pole.

She doesn't read. (Why? she says.) What she wants
most is money, the shiny lie of the mall.
What she wants is out. Tell me the truth, she said one day.
When will we be gone from here?

I'd like to feed her words. Lying on our backs in the dark.
Lower them to her lips. Incarnadine. Rhodopsin. Sweet
droop of them. The promise on her tongue.

But she doesn't want this. Not at all.
The word lasagna is not the thing lasagna
and that's what matters. You eat it and it's gone.

A word doesn't flicker like a bad light bulb
in the stairwell behind you. (You die
and that's it, she would say.)

Is this how we stop belonging to each other?
Humanity and language emptied to private ritual. The
cloistered whispers of love. (But isn't that why
we fall in love anyway, to be able to say the secret,
dangerous words that are in our heads? To name
each other with them in the dark?)

And the opposite of this – how we lose responsibility
for meaning – the blank, common jargon of cults and
talk shows. Words masticated to drool.

We still need language to find us, to tell us where
we are. Radar. The backlit screen. (That's just crap,
she would say.) The truth
is that these words mean it's over,
that already we are gone from here.

Leaving

Planets stir in the blood. Haul of stars
from the throat. Gravity gone and I
confess everything. Out here the sky
utterly ruined, singe along the sea edge,
carmine, raised like braille. I can feel
the shift and spin, the lie of permanence,
sting of evaporate on my skin. This is
what I always feared. The backwards
glance through the sealed window. Spokes
of smoky light. The green-blue wheel of earth
rolling contented and away, without me.

Climatology

My father kept a weather diary.
Rain heavy. Boy to man.
Two continents. *Very cold.*

Pages and days of *Thunder
over the downs* in his
cramped hand, watery blue

ink floating *East wind* as
an island, the seep of it
through the paper.

On May 8, 1945 there's
Rain early and then *Crowds
cheering. The war is over.*

Four entries noting his failure
to pass Aircraft Recognition
but no mention of his

father, shot down over the
Mediterranean in a Lancaster Bomber.
Body never recovered.

Weather can be trusted, its
effect imagined. Take an umbrella.
Wear a hat. *Sunny in Holland.*

Here, snow fell again in the night.
A climate is a language you
learn through your skin.

The grammar of rain. Hot
start of spoken light. The
articulate grief of the sky.

Never seen anything, writes my father,
*so pretty as the sun rising
on snow and ice covered trees.*

Anthem

1.

Tell me a secret. Put your
hand on my heart. The black
flaps on its hinge. Car lights
distant and hard as stars.
Roll a small stone around in my mouth.
Save me or don't, but
arrive sure as morning, the
bright stall of day.
A tangle of light in your hair.

2.

Leap of tall grasses. The cure
of wind. Clouds swab the blue
scrape of sky. Voices climb
from their sleep. Low utterance
of rocky hollow, the shifting agreement
of trees and water. A ligature
of light binds movement to shadow,
wrist to wrist. Press your
certain words to the raw whisper
of my skin. Untie me.

3.

The faith of what is vertical.
The constancy of motion. Lie down,
your body is a river. Walk
towards me holding up the sky.
Touch the upright nerves of the earth,
the hot spit skewer of them turning
in your fingers. Let me take
your charred hands, open as wings,
fold them back into the
fluent waters of your heart.

4.

Moon through chain link. Cross
hatch. Draw this. Love as
keepsake and chaos, the long
diagonal that breaks my body,
lamplight on concrete. Stars
that leak from the skin.
The gap of sky over the railyard,
fill it with the bones of dreams,
luminous and final as music.

5.

Cold tin. Rain polishing the blue
steps. The door closes, empty,
repeatable, a sunken bell. The
failure of what is there. Stone
lintel. Linoleum. The unlit hall.
Sad pulse of fire in the grate.
List of smoke. The way we lean
slowly forward, leave the dead.
The way we leave their forgiveness.

6.

Hatchet of shadow chipping light
from the field. Gnaw
of memory on rib bone. You won't
be back but you haven't
gone. I can still taste
the sweet brine of your name,
hold onto absence with my mouth.
Snow begins its long delay.
The slant of loss. Italic.
Love. Love. Lean on it.

What Is Truly There

That latch of whisper lifting after
feeling through these dark halls at night. My
hand pressing on your breastbone. This
hard. Smooth wall, opening frame of air,
like I could say anything, just once,

like I could fall this far.
The clean stunt of memory. Jump
and be brave about it. Rough wash
of carpet on the landing. I lift
the loose hair from the back of

your neck, like this is what's promised,
like I could give everything away.
Red sways in the leaded glass at
the top of the stairs. Your mouth open
under mine. This slow rise. What is truly gone.

Reunion

I've forgotten more faces than I remember, and everyone's
changed or isn't. The flutter of arbitrary deaths and marriages.

The past stays where it was, that's the deal. Time a shining
ring. Nebula. Marry me. Because I said so. Because it seems

I was the only one seriously necking with the
high school janitor. He was old then, is dead now,

and I'm not sorry for anything. It's a surprise
to still have those kisses, to know my body has been more

faithful than my mind. And I wouldn't have guessed or
wanted that. The press of his chest on mine, sprung camber

of ribs. Grey beard soft on my open mouth. I could feel
his breathing, can feel it now, that particular arch

and fall, how one person's breathing is unlike another's, how
the rhythm of the body sways time and language, moves us out

of our lives and back into them. And I know this now,
only. Let your body remember what it was sure of. We only have

this long. Get it right. Press your ear to these lines, the memory
of me, over here by the furnace in the boiler room, breathing.

Body Double

A woman is the rolling sea. A
woman is the ship. Arms as spars,
stretched out over water that fills
and empties. Breathing. What we know
is true. This moving body,

all the world there is. A woman's
hands are birds, fibrillate
from her wrists, whir and waver.
The sight of them flies up to
the roof of the mouth, quivers

above the tongue. Roses, a roll of roses.
Poured onto this hard earth, dropping
like the sound her moving hands make as wings.
A cascade. Plumage. Water as a body
spilling for another's passage.

The Place That Is You

I should have kissed you years ago,
when we were young and stupid,
thinking that what we wanted had
to happen to us, like an accident,
that we couldn't make our lives ourselves.

Desire is a kind of regret, the reach
of it, the after-burn. I could
still want you, it turns that quickly, flickers.
Strange now to find the space taken up
by the things I never did is the same

as the space filled with those I did, that life
offers equal measure to achievement and wish,
that our mind is our body is our mind.
This solid ground of home and words,
your known and vanished face.

Architecture of the Everyday

House

1.
What is made to fit. What fits.
The confident serrated edge. Key,
the sequel knife. What turns
in the throat, opens as cadence.
Drift of bare floor. The tame coats.
Come into this. Make it right.

2.
The cold night fence. Concrete.
Inside, the painted arch. Gold hooks
by the door, lures for an impossible
moon. Slippery fish of light, mercurial
in the hall. Lift us sudden, arced
and shining, from our lives.

3.
Boots roost in the under stair dark.
On top, the measured rise. As far
as you can go with a hand
on the railing. Wooden stutter. Talk
talk. Through the landing window, a
green silence. The blue delay.

4.
The passageway a hot-wired nerve.
Rooms the chambered corpse. Here
the drawer of private, numbered
griefs. Breath larval on leaded
glass. Doors that articulate
on their hinges. Open in. Open out.

Factory

1.

Harpsichord floor. Warped grain like wires.
Feet scuff music from the wooden sway. Dead
bird, dead bird. Sticky light coagulates on the
loose pipe. Horn pipe. This is
everything you've wanted. Dance band.

2.

Strap of light. Harness maker. Blunt canter
of hammer on leather, I told you so.
The swing of hope, how it swings as
an arm coming down, how the sun's coming
down. This far into the room.

3.
Weight in the same place, always, and now
a creaky floor by the window. Our
real ghosts, these buildings we have taught
to remember us. The clank of our machines,
our hearts. The unforgiven view.

4.
The way we crossed the room, which wall
was leant against. This is open, here,
relief of stairs. Don't go. Don't let me.
Map of water on the ceiling. Air
that bends around us still. Footfall.

Port

1.

All day the ships wait, shiver in the flat
pan of water, compass needles, aligned and hopeful.
Let us be where we think we are. Radio
wave. Who's out there? In the dark they're lanterns
swinging with the tide, soldering a welt of sky.
Night burns shut. We're here, here. Come back to us.

2.

Unravel. Undone. The bridge spools across the harbour.
Rock sprockets. Loss flaps over the lens of water,
shiny and translucent. Look right through this. Look
down. Memory a lacuna. The tanker moving into
light tipped with roses. Don't lift your eyes. This
is all there is. What you have.

3.

Sulphur puckers, stark yellow, lecherous. Cicatrice
of smoke above the docks. Abrade. Step
back. Up close, the crumbling sky. Cargo
rocks and lowers. What was never said. The pulpy
sky fermenting off the point. The lethal
air. I'm here. Let it go.

Suburbs

1.

Dashboard light. Aura burning green. Halo, the
neon buzz of the beer store, here where stars
are always literal, glisten in the hard black
stone of heaven. We're done for. We know this.

2.

Stairwell. Car lot. My hands shake when
I touch you. Hot steel. The lake edge
wound tight around the trees, blue string.
Say that I never left, always it was me.

3.

Build over the sad spaces, the memory of houses. A
tangle of lilac by an absent front door. Everything
we are, gone, even while we're here. The lurch
of headlights. This darkened street.

Stairwell

We're here and not. The hollow we fall
out of when we wake, someone's voice
calling for us not to go. Familiar,
where am I? The known velocity,
footsteps overhead, the tamping of gauzy breath
into the cracked and brittle air.
What detonates in the space between where
we are and where we
are? Echo or answer? The lit fuse
hisses in our mouths. We're not saying anything.
Go on. Take it back.

Roof

Up and up. Bone bloat of the moon
over water. Ladder of trees bent against
sky. The shingle is a rough tongue, hooks
into skin, scrapes like a promise certain
to be broken. Promise it will be broken.
Brick, the chimney, smoke untying. Rising.
Where what burns goes. The heat
from words. The heat from the clenched
earth at night. Each rooftop a dark
tarpaulin hung from faulty stars.
Each breath ascending.

Window

From outside, the lit rooms stack and
collapse, like words while they're being said,
how wings fold to a wall.
And what you see here, stiff brocade,
tarnish, is not what I meant. Even
the desk upstairs with your picture on it
is a lie. The stretch of shadows
on this page, elastic as forgiveness. Listen.
Our fidelity is not to light but to
our memory of it. We're looking
for words we want to hear.

Arch

Roof of the mouth. The ordinary words
that go on ahead of us, through the fleeting
dialect of roses, under stone.
We walk into what we say, surprised
by sudden brightness, hands feeling
for the hard, smooth prayer. What
all this is, moving into spaces our words
have left. The firefighter ready to enter
the burning building. I'm gone, he says,
as he steps through the doorway.
And he is.

August

Buildings fall back, out of their shadows.
Fine etch of memory. Bricks and
measured glass. The cold stumble of
twilight through a window.

It won't go any further than this.
Grief pushed to the back of the throat,
swallowed with a glass of water. What
is over winching its name open,

once more, before winter. Shy light
holding above the factory. The surprise
of longing on your tongue. Just that,
and smoke like a word you used to know.

After a Poem by Elizabeth Bishop

Through a mesh of kisses, falling rain
on the roof. The clear feel of this minute,
electric and sudden, air hissing with light.
To wake together, the same rain, what
our bodies hear. Pass of wires over the flat roof,
a net thrown up to catch the black sky.

The house struck down, go on, imagine this.
The moving storm, prickle of sweat
at the back of your neck. We are caught,
here in the blue air lightning shreds.
Bird cage. Rattle of song. The sky
wakes from the dream of us, runs electric.

A kiss is never simple, that's the point.
Lie down. The flat black back of night
above us, roof, thick wires of darkness
coiled in the room. It's always been this easy
and this hard to love. Ourselves no
different, the world completely changed.

After a Poem by Louise Bogan

The silence that we come from
is not strength or virtue. To
have no image for this is not
to love. Time forgets us anyway,
absorbs our secrets and our mettle,
moulds our bodies to earth, to air,
turns us from purpose. No one
inherits who we are. Your hand

in mine is a pressure, a truth
that will not last outside of this,
unless we keep it here, match
it to an image, put it down
as rhyme. What is beautiful
should make a sound, should ring.
If I cannot give you that, then
I cannot give you anything.

After a Poem by Sylvia Plath

Cut throats. Burnt metal. All night
I have tasted this dream. It assembles in
nerves like poison, stiffens into place, noiseless,
obstructs the real sky, gray trees, the stilled
Chevrolet, that stone lawn. This winter dawn
a line of tin hammered onto the green wheel
of the sea. I slow-roll out of this, move back
into the colour of things, the hush of sun

beautiful on the balconies. This bed, this room.
Space melting into space. The echoes of light.
The unbuckled sea. I have come out
entirely, soul and bones, terror opened to
a view of clapboard and rubber plants, the
peeled earth in front of houses, patched roofs.
How hard sometimes to tell the guest from the host,
to know what disappears and what remains.

Yaddo

Say that again, more than anything.

The tower inside is like a bell under water.
Pines sway, dark and submerged in the April
morning beyond the window.

The roses are over. The gardens are sleeping.
Each statue stopped with a wooden box, the mansion
boarded up. One day snow upon the verandah,
the next day ice, the next one water – as though
what is uttered each night is each day forgiven.

Lakes glitter green through the trees, fish scales
flexed with light.

There are twelve of us here. We are cheerful
at meals, happy to be together in this place
where art doesn't need to be explained or defended.

Three of us have seen the fox, and I have seen
two people kissing in a blue car by the racetrack.
We have all seen the comet that won't be back

for 2,000 years, a swatch of light wiped across
the dark sleeve of sky between the pines.

We are the ghosts here. These books, these chairs
are what remains after we have vanished. This
room in West House that rings gold with
afternoon sun. Walk in and it could be
any year. You could be anyone.
To be here is to be gone.

Say it again. I have wanted this.
More than anything.

Joshua Tree

This is the human landscape, one without water,
where we can feel our bodies dry and sift
to grit in the sun, where all the shapes
of erosion – boulders and hollows – can be
made with knuckle, fist, fluent hand.

Here, light pools in the valleys, hefts a
channel between rock to flow through. Blue
buoyant sky. A backlit rabbit on the path
to the car, ears shimmering translucent,
light sponging through its flimsy skin.

It isn't the sea in us, but this place, where
we are the roll and swagger, rise and
shudder, the moving thing. Where we become
this light, a light so pure that it
drips, drips down, spills as water.

The Anatomy of Trees

1.
What can't be seen at night: the pale
pink of roses. Anything blue.

Colour is not constant. Nothing
that holds colour can be relied on.

At night what is distinguished is not light
or dark, but lighter or darker.

2.
Walking up through trees
the forest is a green furnace,
covers us completely, our breath
sparks in the embered air.

Along the ridge, burnt trees are a line
of black fence, limbs stunted
by fire, more skeletal than bone.
An accent of scorched sky between them.

They are still in place among the living,
those trees. We put everything
in the ground and think
it's really gone.

3.
Green lanterns swing above the river, green
light stretching over water. The air
flushed with effort. The sun going down.

We come from this, and I forget it.
Straight lines of trees, salt curve of water.
A singular knowledge. A common prayer.

Evening light tastes of roses.

False Alarms

Behind steel doors I sit up
all night with the machines.
Codes and silences. Burglary, panic,
fire. I send out the sirens,
banshees in the quiet streets,
winding back the tin roofs of the suburbs.

Later, they'll all be false. The drunk
old woman in the penthouse who invented
her heart attack. A cat walking through
a motion detector. Wind down the chimney.
The wife of the judge, locked out
of the house by him, naked, breaking
back in through the basement window.

In my sealed room I imagine movement.
Five minutes in a living room to trash it, pile
up the TV and stereo in the hall.
Quick hands skidding over furniture, still
on the smooth wood of a door frame as new
rooms open like breath, like promises.
What is truly valuable, small enough to carry.

Someone slamming reckless through me, knowing
what to look for, what might be there
for them to have. Every lover is a thief.
Tell me. Who that rescues doesn't also
dream of being saved?

Witness

What you think of as the soldiers
search the barn where you are hiding,
to rape and kill and rape you,
is how easily the thread
of your breathing comes undone,
unravels in the cool morning air.

What you hold onto is the sweet
living smell of your own skin,
the finger of blue sky through the barnboards,
the memory of your mother's voice.

If it is a poem it is not this one.
It is words you still believe,
ones you can die inside.
There is no comfort here. You
won't reach for these words –
this poem that wants
to tell your story,
that thinks your story is
just what happened to you.

Beneath the Sea

You've just gone, stepped down
off the seaplane ramp
into the Atlantic. The metallic husk
of your breathing still
shearing the air.

Out across the water, mist sheds its skin
onto the hills, is a word we're always
looking for, one we can't get right. Sloughs,
now it sloughs. Here, wet rusted tongue,
light that slops down like dishwater,
gray and soupy. You're beneath the sea
and I'm walking through this ruined hangar,
glass popping like sniper fire
under my boots.

Crabs, you say later. Big crabs and
clouds of broken-backed shrimp. I
lay down in the grass.

Come up.
Come up now.

Inside the hangar the concrete floor is smooth sand
on the bottom of the ocean
where my grandfather is cold salt bones in his plane.
What is left of us. All the stories
of how we fall from the sky.

For one whole summer, when
my sister is eight, she tries to walk
on the fetid scum of the backyard pool.

I remember when I was like you, says my mother.

Shrug. The word for how the fog creeps
down the hills. A shrug of fog.

Do we ever get it right?

This is how we mostly live, not on land but
between ocean and sky, in the wreckage of the past.
In the bombed-out hollows light carves
from rock and water, death and motion.
Our sun a poisoned apple. Our bodies
choked with fire, burning fuselage.

Out here, by the seaplane ramp, I wait for you to
surface. It is never that simple.
The distant hills are slurred with mist.

There you are.

Foxes

I'm reading poems by a woman who wrote about
her death before she knew she was dying. Poetry
rises as memory, comes down as prophesy.

What I wanted was to tell the story of the foxes.
The drive up, before dawn, to see the sun rise
behind the lighthouse. How the two foxes circled us

in the parking lot, one jumping onto the car and peeing,
staring at us through the windshield, defiant and sure,
red fur lit with wind. How afterwards everyone

said this shouldn't have happened, this behaviour, these
foxes at the lighthouse. But I don't know where
to end this story, and what I'm really doing is

reading, not writing. Better to be in the dead poet's
poems about haystacks and pears, than to be here,
in the mountains, or to be here, in the poem.

In the mountains early snow has blanched the summer
grass and the woods at night blaze like an x-ray.
In the poem there are black rocks by the road

as we drive up to the lighthouse. Blossoms of fog
bloom once, lush and flawless against the glass.
There we tried to read the foamy alphabet

of the sea; the cold, salt air tasting of secrets.
We wanted the right word for everything. Here,
the dead poet talks about the woods, but they're not

these woods. Reading her puts me where I am and
takes me from there too. The pull of it
like wanting. (Ten years ago I would have said

desire, but that's not it.) Wanting is a word that fills
and empties, a word that, like the sea, remembers
itself each time differently.

At first we were certain the foxes were a warning.
Then we thought that somehow they were us. The
menace was ourselves, each other. Now I think

it's all true. There was a sluice of light
behind them on the hills as they ran through the dry
grass, away from us. And you have gone now,

just as swiftly. Well, goodbye. I want to say
that what we did, trying to name the fog on the hills,
was like writing, but not as lonely. It was like

reading, not lonely at all. And the foxes?
What they've become now are words – these ones, the ones
of the dead poet. They circled us and left us.

Grief and consolation. Mercy, mercy, like a rope of stars.
This is the space between fire and sea, between
what I know and what I can say.

And I have always told myself that I live
for this – what comes for me
and is not mine.

Reading

'You have put your two hands upon me, and your mouth,
You have said my name as a prayer.' – Louise Bogan

The bad poet is reading and I'm looking
out the window, down at the park where I
walk the dog, wishing us through the grove of firs,
past the hollow where we hid once in a storm,
the dog digging us a pit to lie in
because she thought we lived there now.

The bad poet has a poem for every time she's had
a feeling. There was one in California and
another in Toronto. She had the same feeling
twice in Mexico, when it rained.

Out of the trees the dog waits on the hill
for the distant shapes along the river path
to run themselves into dogs. Then she's down
the slope and gone to them. Each day her
purpose renewed and rewarded, to make herself again
into what she knows herself to be.

I have this dog because I once read a poet
who wrote about walking up through the birch wood
with her dog, about how when she was depressed
the dog's breathing was a simple prayer, shunting
meaning back into her life.

That poet is dead now, and we're all ascending
up through the birch wood, out of the twentieth
century, leaving them behind, those writers who
mended my life in small, permanent ways.

Goodbye, goodbye. Jane, Virginia, Anne. Language
is the shelter you prepared for me. This is where
we used to live. Goodbye to the poet whose book
I adored, who answered my awkward letter.
My Love, she said.

Coda

Molten grass, ridged like lava. Mist breathing
above the water. Open this from anywhere.
The world on fire, greasy orange, cascading
down the hills, something that happens in the back
of your throat. Or the gauzy whisper of
morning overheard from shore, ghostly
and specific. I went away. I came back.

The trees like spines. The woods still
green. You will never be here. Push back
wet branches, the lace of ferns
patterning your boots. Alone with
someone else's words. But this is what
there is to believe in. Go on, imagine
this is me. I'll imagine this is you.

'So you see Love, love: and it's
the last day of the year by the way.'
    – Virginia Woolf

Notes

The Canadian Tire trucks in 'Narrative' are for Mary Louise Adams.

'Variations' is for Martin Humphreys.

'After a Poem by Elizabeth Bishop' is a transposition (i.e. using most of the same words in my poem as she used in hers, but subverting the order and meaning) of Elizabeth Bishop's 'It is marvellous to wake up together,' which was first published, posthumously, in *Elizabeth Bishop: The Biography of a Poetry*, by Lorrie Goldensohn.

'After a Poem by Louise Bogan' is a transposition of Louise Bogan's 'Poem in Prose.'

'After a Poem by Sylvia Plath' is a transposition of Sylvia Plath's 'Waking in Winter.'

The imagery in 'Body Double' is taken from, and inspired by, the dance choreography of Crystal Pite and Hope Terry – specifically 'Inside Passage' by Crystal Pite, and 'At a Loss' by Hope Terry.

The title and some of the information in the poem 'The Anatomy of Trees' is taken from *The Artistic Anatomy of Trees* by Rex Vicat Cole, published by Seely, Service & Co. Ltd. in 1915. This poem is for Mary Louise Adams.

The second 'Beneath the Sea' and 'Foxes' are for Elise Levine.

The Louise Bogan quote in the poem 'Reading' is taken from her poem 'Betrothed.'

The quote from Virginia Woolf at the end of the book is taken from a letter she wrote to Vita Sackville-West on December 31st, 1928.

While I was working on this book, I was inspired and influenced by many books of poetry, particularly *Song* by Brigit Pegeen Kelly, *Otherwise* by Jane Kenyon, *Aurora* by Sharon Thesen, *Mean Time* by Carol Ann Duffy, *The Dream of the Unified Field* by Jorie Graham, *Land To Light On* by Dionne Brand, *WSW (West South West)* by Erin Mouré, *The Lord and the General Din of the World* by Jane Mead, *Red Trousseau* by Carol Muske, *The Angel of History* by Carolyn Forché, *The First Four Books of Poems* by Louise Glück, and *Connecting the Dots* by Maxine Kumin. The debt I owe these poets, both as a reader and a writer, is incalculable.

Acknowledgements

I would like to thank the editors of *The Canadian Forum* and *The Fiddlehead* where some of these poems were published.

For financial assistance during the writing of this book I am grateful to the Canada Council and the Regional Municipality of Ottawa-Carleton. For the luxury of uninterrupted time I would like to thank the Leighton Studios, Banff Centre for the Arts, and the Corporation of Yaddo for residencies.

Thanks to Elise Levine, and to Nadine McInnis for reading an earlier draft of these poems and offering her fine editorial advice. Thanks to the Ottawa poets for those brunches, and for making me feel welcome while I lived in Ottawa.

As always, thanks to Mary Louise Adams. And Hazel.

Thanks to Betty Goodwin for allowing me to use her work on the cover of this book. Thanks also to René Blouin at Galerie René Blouin for facilitating this process.

Thanks to everyone at Brick.

I would especially like to thank my editor, Clare Goulet, for her acumen, thoroughness, and good humour. It was a pleasure to work with her and *Anthem* is a much better book because of her efforts.

Helen Humphreys is the author of three previous books of poetry: *Gods and Other Mortals* (Brick Books, 1986), *Nuns Looking Anxious, Listening to Radios* (Brick Books, 1990), and *The Perils of Geography* (Brick Books, 1995). Her novel *Leaving Earth* (HarperCollins, 1997) has been published in nine countries and won the 1998 City of Toronto Book Award. She lives and writes in Kingston, Ontario.